Social media giants are poisoning our journalism, our politics, our relationships and ultimately our minds. Glenn Reynolds looks at the up and downsides of social media and at proposals for regulation, and offers his own fix that respects free speech while reducing social media's toll.

GLENN HARLAN REYNOLDS is the Beauchamp Brogan Distinguished Professor of Law at the University of Tennessee. He blogs at Instapundit.com and writes for such publications as the Atlantic, Forbes, Popular Mechanics, the Wall Street Journal, and USA Today. He lives in Knoxville, Tennessee.

The information world is undergoing a transformation, and it's huge.

How huge? Huge enough that its impact is comparable to the introduction of agriculture, with similarly far-reaching effects on human civilization. And like the introduction of agriculture, though its impact may be positive overall, there will be significant costs along with the benefits, and neither the costs nor the benefits will be borne evenly.

In this short book, I will look at the change in communications technology that has taken place over the past couple of centuries, and particularly over the past couple of decades. I will explore both the benefits and the downsides of these changes, and look at what's likely to come next. I will also look at efforts to ameliorate the downsides through regulation of online speech and other approaches. I will conclude with some suggestions of my own.

The Change

Society seems to be growing steadily crazier. And maybe it doesn't just seem to be. Maybe it actually *is* growing crazier. Science-fiction writer Robert Heinlein's 1930s future history dubbed the early 21st century "the Crazy Years," a time when rapid technological and social change would leave people psychologically unmoored and, well, crazy. Today's society seems to be living up to that prediction. But why?

I recently read James C. Scott's *Against the Grain: A Deep History of the Earliest States,* and one of the interesting aspects of the earliest agricultural civilizations is how fragile they were. A bunch of people and their animals would crowd together in a newly formed city, and diseases that weren't much of a threat when everybody was out hunting and gathering over large areas would suddenly spread like wildfire and depopulate the town almost overnight.

As Scott writes, an early city was more like a (badly run) refugee resettlement camp than a modern urban area, with people thrown together higgledy-piggledy with no real efforts at sanitation or amenities. He observes that "the pioneers who created this historically novel ecology could not possibly have known the disease vectors they were inadvertently unleashing."

Then I ran across this observation on Twitter: "The Internet is rewiring brains and social relations. Could it be producing a civilizational nervous breakdown?" And I saw another article noting that depression in teens skyrocketed between 2010 and 2015, as smartphones took over. It made me wonder if we're in the same boat as the Neolithic cities, only for what you might call viruses of the mind: toxic ideas and emotions that spread like wildfire.

Maybe we don't know the mental-disease vectors that we're inadvertently unleashing, just as those early civilizations didn't understand the physical-disease vectors they were promoting. Looking around at today's society, that certainly seems plausible.

Hunters and gatherers were at far less risk for infectious disease because they didn't encounter very many new people very often. Their exposure was low, and contact among such bands was sporadic enough that diseases couldn't spread very fast. Their environment and lifestyle were such that both diseases and ideas spread slowly.

It wasn't until you crowded thousands or tens of thousands of them, along with their animals, into small dense areas with poor sanitation that disease outbreaks took off. Instead of meeting dozens of new people per year, an urban dweller probably encountered hundreds per day. Diseases that would have affected only a few people at a time as they spread slowly across a continent (or just burned out for lack of new carriers) would now, in these congested urban centers, leap from person to person in a flash. It's no surprise that the earliest cities often depopulated themselves via epidemics.

Likewise, in recent years we've gone from an era when ideas spread comparatively slowly to one in which social media, in particular, allow them to spread like wildfire. A few hundred years ago, ideas spread mainly by word of mouth, or by books, which had to travel physically. Later they spread via newspapers. Now they spread at the speed of light, and are shared almost as quickly, at the click of a mouse.

Sometimes that's good, when they're good ideas. But most ideas are probably bad. Maybe we don't know the mental-disease vectors that we're inadvertently unleashing, just as those early civilizations didn't understand the physical-disease vectors they were promoting. Looking around at today's society, that certainly seems plausible.

It took three things to help control the spread of disease in cities: sanitation, acclimation, and better nutrition. In early cities, after all, people had no idea how diseases spread, something we didn't fully understand until the late 19th century. But rule-of-thumb sanitation made things a lot better over time. Also, populations eventually adapted: Diseases became endemic, not epidemic, and usually less severe as people developed immunity. And finally, as Scott notes, surviving disease was always a function of nutrition, with better-nourished populations doing much better than malnourished ones.

Right now, it almost seems as if the social media world was designed to spread viruses of the mind. And that's probably because it was. While in the earlier days of the Internet ideas spread faster than before, today in the walled gardens of social media outlets like Facebook, Instagram, or especially Twitter, ideas spread much, much faster, and with less time for rumination or consideration, than ever before. And that's by design, as social media companies use algorithms that promote posts based on "engagement" – which typically means users' emotional reactions – and "share" buttons allow each user to pass them on to hundreds or thousands of friends, who can then do the same. This repeated sharing and resharing can produce a chain reaction reminiscent of a nuclear reactor with the control rods removed.

As Jaron Lanier writes, "Engagement is not meant to serve any particular purpose other than its own enhancement, and yet the result is an unnatural global amplification of the 'easy' emotions, which happen to be the negative ones.... Remember, with old-fashioned advertising you could measure whether a product did better after an ad was run, but now companies are measuring whether individuals changed their behaviors, and the feeds for each person are constantly tweaked to get individual behavior to change.... The scheme I am describing amplifies negative emotions more than positive ones, so it's more efficient at harming society than at improving it."

In the newspaper age, a full day passed from one pub-lication to the next, and newspapers had to physically travel from the printing plant to the readers. It was possible to share newspaper articles, but only to a relatively small number of friends. Even with the advent of television and radio, there was usually a similar time, days or at least hours, between programs, and sharing was basically impos-sible. Ideas spread quickly, by historical standards, but not with anything like the speed of today's social media.

This increase in speed, along with some other charac-teristics of social media, has led to calls for stricter speech regulation. In the pages that follow, I will outline some argu-ments for such regulation, suggest some counterarguments, and then offer some suggested responses of my own.

In short, criticisms of social media as speech fall into several categories: it is too fast, it is too incomplete, it is too emotional, and it is too untrustworthy. All of these claims have some merit.

Too Fast

For most of human history, ideas spread slowly. They could travel no faster than the human being sharing them, and the only way they could be transferred was word of mouth. Some ideas still did well: Homer's work, for example, spread in exactly this fashion. But it was slow at best, and Homer is perhaps the exception that proves the rule, as comparatively little thinking from the preliterate era survives.

The invention of writing, and later of printing, meant that ideas could spread much more widely. Their speed was still limited by human speeds of travel (though such speed was improving a bit) but circulation no longer required word-of-mouth contact. A book, handbill, or newspaper

Right now, it almost seems as if the social media world was designed to spread viruses of the mind. And that's probably because it was.

could reach multiple readers, and once movable type arrived post-Gutenberg it was easy to produce them in comparatively large numbers.

Thomas Paine's pamphlet *Common Sense* was the best-selling work of the Colonial era; it sold 100,000 copies in 1776, the year it was published. Given that the population of the United States was 2.5 million at the time, that's quite impressive. If we assume, plausibly, given that copies were distributed and read aloud at taverns and other public places, that each copy was perused by five people, that would mean that 20 percent of the American population — and a much higher percentage of the adult population, of course – was exposed to Paine's work in its first year. This is huge, but, of course, it was also an exceptional case.

The spread of information got faster throughout the 19th century, as railroads increased the speed of travel dramatically, and the telegraph meant that, for the first time, information could travel long distances much, much faster than a human could. Multiple editions of newspapers in big cities meant that an idea published in a morning edition could, at least in principle, be responded to or repeated in an afternoon paper. And with the invention of radio and television, ideas could be broadcast to many people – not simply, as with the telegraph, from point to point – at the speed of light.

This represented a major increase in speed of transmission, but the speed of interaction was still comparatively slow. Television or radio news broadcasts were scheduled things, not really interactive with one another, and, most importantly, they were *broadcasts,* information spread outward from a single point. They were important new technologies, for good or for evil (Hitler's mastery of radio was a major part of his success) but they still gave people time to ruminate and think about what they broadcast. And these broadcasts weren't prone to near-instantaneous chain reactions.

Even the Internet made less of a difference, at first, than

it might have. Originally, Internet news was just newspaper content ported over to a website. "Newsgroups" on Usenet were probably the first truly interactive medium, in which any individual could post items and everyone else could respond instantaneously. Usenet quickly gained a reputation for "flame wars" and the promulgation of conspiracy theories, which in retrospect probably should have been a warning.

Even the "blogosphere" of the early 21st century, in which independently run blog sites posted items on news and responded both to Big Media stories and to each other, was more like traditional media in some respects than like Usenet or social media. To read content on blogs, readers had to go there. To interact, bloggers had to read each other's sites and decide to post a response, generally with a link back to the post they were replying to. If you didn't like a blog you could just ignore it. A story that spread like wildfire through the blogosphere still did so over the better part of a day, not over minutes, and it was typically pretty easy to find the original item and get context, something the culture of blogging encouraged. (As James Lileks wrote, "The link changes everything. When someone derides or exalts a piece, the link lets you examine the thing itself, without interference." And bloggers often encouraged their readers to follow the link and – to use a popular blogospheric phrase – "read the whole thing.") In addition, a story's spreading required at least a modicum of actual thought and consideration on the part of bloggers, who were also constrained, to a greater or lesser degree, by considerations of reputation. Some blogs served as trusted nodes on the blogosphere, and many other bloggers would be reluctant to run with a story that the trusted nodes didn't believe.

In engineering parlance, the early blogosphere was a "loosely coupled" system, one where changes in one part were not immediately or directly transmitted to others. Loosely coupled systems tend to be resilient, and not very subject to systemic failures, because what happens in one part of the system affects other parts only weakly and slowly.

Tightly coupled systems, on the other hand, where changes affecting one node swiftly affect others, are prone to cascading failures. Usenet was one such system, where an entire newsgroup could be ruined by a spreading "flame war." If a blogger flamed, people could just ignore the blog; when a Usenet user flamed, others got sucked in until the channel was filled with people yelling at each other. (As Nick Denton wrote, the blogosphere "routes around idiots" in a way that Usenet didn't, because the blogosphere doesn't depend on the common channel that a Usenet group did.)

Social media – especially Twitter – is more like Usenet than blogs, but in many ways is worse. Like Usenet, it is tightly coupled. The "retweet," "comment," and "like" buttons are immediate. A retweet sends a posting, no matter how angry or misinformed, to all the retweeter's followers, who can then do the same to their followers, and so on, in a runaway chain reaction. Unlike blogs, little to no thought is required, and in practice very few people even follow the link (if there is one) to "read the whole thing." According to a study by computer scientists at Columbia University and the French National Institute, 59 percent of people who share a link on social media don't read the underlying story. (I'm honestly surprised the number isn't higher.)

As Caitlin Dewey reported in *The Washington Post*:

> Worse, the study finds that these sort of blind peer-to-peer shares are really important in determining what news gets circulated and what just fades off the public radar. So your thoughtless retweets, and those of your friends, are actually shaping our shared political and cultural agendas.
>
> "People are more willing to share an article than read it," study co-author Arnaud Legout said in a statement. "This is typical of modern information consumption. People form an opinion based on a summary,

or a summary of summaries, without making the effort
to go deeper."

To verify that depressing piece of conventional Internet wisdom, Legout and his co-authors collected two data sets: the first, on all tweets containing Bit.ly-shortened links to five major news sources during a one-month period last summer; the second, on all of the clicks attached to that set of shortened links, as logged by Bit.ly, during the same period. After cleaning and collating that data, the researchers basically found themselves with a map to how news goes viral on Twitter.

And that map showed, pretty clearly, that "viral" news is widely shared — but not necessarily, you know, read.

Commenting on this study in *Forbes*, Jayson DeMers writes:

The circulation of headlines in this way leads to an echo
chamber effect. Users are more likely to share headlines
that adhere to their pre-existing conceptions, rather
than challenging them, and as a result, publishers try
to post more headlines along those lines. Social groups
regurgitate the same types of posts and content over
and over again, leading to a kind of information

stagnation. This is one of the most powerful negative repercussions of the blind sharing effect.

This trend also makes it easier for journalists and content publishers to manipulate their audiences – whether they intend to or not. In a headline, one small word change can make a big difference, and even if you report all the real facts in the body of your article, the way you shape a headline can completely transform how users interpret your presentation of information. This is a dangerous and powerful tool.

That's exactly right. Social media makes people less informed but more partisan.

The "block" and "mute" functions on Twitter, and similar tools on Facebook, etc., are intended to protect against Usenet-style flame wars, but to the extent that they work, they also put people in bubbles of similar thinkers, which tends to encourage the spread of misinformation so long as it matches the thinkers' prejudices. This problem is particularly severe as research indicates that a majority of people get their news from social media. According to a 2017 Pew

Social media makes people less informed but more partisan.

study, 67 percent of Americans get at least some of their news from social media, and even among older Americans (those over 50) more than half rely on social media for a significant part of their news diet.

Twitter in particular seems prone to waves of viral misinformation or hatred, which spread much faster, and with far less critical thinking, than anything we saw in the blogosphere. The result has been a series of pile-ons involving people whose alleged misbehavior (which often turns out to be fictional, or misrepresented) winds up costing them their jobs.

The archetypical example involved PR executive Justine Sacco, who tweeted to her 170 followers as she got ready to board a flight to South Africa: "Going to Africa. Hope I don't get AIDS. Just kidding. I'm white!" She then got on the plane, turned off her phone, and while airborne and out of touch became the number one topic on Twitter, under the hashtag #HasJustineLandedYet. Although she meant it as a joke about Westerners' paranoia, it produced a shame mob – with help from Gawker Media's Sam Biddle, who admitted he promoted the shaming in search of traffic – that cost her her job.

Such shame mobs have become more common, typically involving nonpublic figures caught out by a

thoughtless or out-of-context statement, as the characteristics of Twitter seem ideally designed for bringing
together an angry mob on short notice. Describing the
phenomenon in *The New York Times,* once-enthusiastic
shamer Jon Ronson had second thoughts:

> [*At first,*] *it felt as if hierarchies were being dismantled,
> as if justice were being democratized. As time passed,
> though, I watched these shame campaigns multiply,
> to the point that they targeted not just powerful insti-
> tutions and public figures but really anyone perceived
> to have done something offensive. I also began to
> marvel at the disconnect between the severity of the
> crime and the gleeful savagery of the punishment. It
> almost felt as if shamings were now happening for
> their own sake, as if they were following a script.*
>
> *Eventually I started to wonder about the recipients
> of our shamings, the real humans who were the virtual
> targets of these campaigns. So for the past two years,
> I've been interviewing individuals like Justine Sacco:
> everyday people pilloried brutally, most often for post-
> ing some poorly considered joke on social media.
> Whenever possible, I have met them in person, to truly
> grasp the emotional toll at the other end of our screens.*

The people I met were mostly unemployed, fired for
their transgressions, and they seemed broken some-
how – deeply confused and traumatized.

And it gets worse:

I met a man who, in early 2013, had been sitting at a
conference for tech developers in Santa Clara, Calif.,
when a stupid joke popped into his head. It was about
the attachments for computers and mobile devices
that are commonly called dongles. He murmured the
joke to his friend sitting next to him, he told me. "It was
so bad, I don't remember the exact words," he said.
"Something about a fictitious piece of hardware that has
a really big dongle, a ridiculous dongle.... It wasn't
even conversation-level volume."
 Moments later, he half-noticed when a woman one
row in front of them stood up, turned around and took
a photograph. He thought she was taking a crowd shot,
so he looked straight ahead, trying to avoid ruining
her picture. It's a little painful to look at the photo-
graph now, knowing what was coming.
 The woman had, in fact, overheard the joke. She
considered it to be emblematic of the gender imbalance
that plagues the tech industry and the toxic, male-

dominated corporate culture that arises from it. She tweeted the picture to her 9,209 followers with the caption: "Not cool. Jokes about ... 'big' dongles right behind me." Ten minutes later, he and his friend were taken into a quiet room at the conference and asked to explain themselves. A day later, his boss called him into his office, and he was fired.

"I packed up all my stuff in a box," he told me. (Like Stone and Sacco, he had never before talked on the record about what happened to him. He spoke on the condition of anonymity to avoid further damaging his career.) "I went outside to call my wife. I'm not one to shed tears, but" – he paused – "when I got in the car with my wife I just.... I've got three kids. Getting fired was terrifying."

The woman who took the photograph, Adria Richards, soon felt the wrath of the crowd herself. The man responsible for the dongle joke had posted about losing his job on Hacker News, an online forum popular with developers. This led to a backlash from the other end of the political spectrum. So-called men's rights activists and anonymous trolls bombarded Richards with death threats on Twitter and Facebook. Someone tweeted Richards's home address along with a photograph of a beheaded woman with duct tape over her *mouth. Fearing for her life, she left her home, sleeping on friends' couches for the remainder of the year.*

When people organize spontaneously, it can be a good thing – look at the GoFundMe campaigns for people who are sick or injured, or disaster responses like the Cajun Navy. But this sort of spontaneous organization seems more like casual cruelty. It's almost like a high-tech version of Shirley Jackson's horror story *The Lottery,* in which a village randomly chooses one of its members to be stoned to death. The rapid-response character of social media lends itself to this sort of thing, which is why it is becoming more common. Meanwhile, in other parts of the world, social media is used not only to persecute individuals, but whole groups, by promoting religious and racial persecution. Twitter CEO Jack Dorsey recently came under fire for ignoring the role of social media (something for which Facebook apologized) in the persecution of Burma's Rohingya people.

Sometimes too-swift reactions are a reason to regulate speech. Traditionally, "incitement" is a category of speech that gets less (or no) First Amendment protection. The classic example of incitement is when a mob, already riled up and emotional, is urged by a speaker to do something violent or illegal right away. This "imminence" is an essential part of incitement, because it means that there won't be time for measured reflection, or even time for someone to try to talk people out of acting. The too-fast characteristics of speech under social media like Twitter would seem to be similar.

I'm not suggesting that tweets and other social media speech should be taken out of First Amendment protection because they are incitement – the full test for incitement, from *Brandenburg v. Ohio,* requires that the speech be intended to produce, and be likely to produce, imminent lawless action. In practice, it's pretty hard for a tweet to promote imminent lawless action since the speaker and the listener are in different physical locations, and listeners aren't likely to do much of anything concrete and immediate in response to a tweet, since they'd have to look up from their phones first. But the notion that speech of the sort that by its nature encourages people to respond without thinking is more problematic than speech that does not seems to me to carry over.

Too Incomplete

Traditional news stories leave a lot out. To boil down events into 800 or 1,000 words – or, increasingly, 500 words – requires omitting a lot of context, history, and background.

In fact, the corruption of the political/intellectual class by social media is particularly serious, since their descent into thoughtless polarization can then spread to the rest of the population, even that large part that doesn't use social media itself, through traditional channels.

But when a news story is presented on Facebook or (especially) Twitter, often only the headline is read, along with, perhaps, a one-sentence summary, as we've seen. Relatively few people click through to read the actual story, which often contains far more information and nuance than the headline, which is usually deliberately provocative.

In his insightful essay *In The Beginning was the Command Line,* Neal Stephenson wrote that, "The ability to think rationally is pretty rare, even in prestigious universities. We're in the TV age now, and people think by linking pictures in their brains." That was 1999. To some degree it's still true, but the pictures have been replaced by catchphrases and hashtags. The short-form character of social media tends to reinforce this.

Even before the rise of social media, critics were worrying that the Internet was shortening people's attention spans. In his work *The Shallows: What the Internet Is Doing to Our Brains,* Nicholas Carr wrote that prior centuries' technological change had worked to encourage people to think longer and harder than in the past. The rise of printed books, which could present arguments and marshal facts on a scale previously unknown, actually changed how people thought and argued.

"The arguments in books became longer and clearer, as well as more complex and more challenging, as writers strived self-consciously to refine their ideas and their logic.... The advances in book technology changed the personal experience of reading and writing. They also had social consequences." The widespread process of deep, attentive reading, Carr writes, changed people and changed society. "The literary mind," he writes, "once confined to the cloisters of the monastery and the towers of the university had become the general mind.... The words in books didn't just strengthen people's ability to think abstractly, they enriched people's experience of the physical world, the world outside the books."

All that has changed, he writes, in the Internet age, a claim that seems surely to be stronger today than a decade ago. "Dozens of studies by psychologists, neurobiologists, educators and Web designers point to the same conclusion: When we go online, we enter an environment that promotes cursory reading, hurried and distracted thinking, and superficial learning. It's possible to think deeply while surfing the Net, just as it's possible to think shallowly while reading a book, but that's not the type of thinking the technology encourages and rewards."

Neuroscientist Maryanne Wolf of UCLA wondered just how social media was affecting us, so she experimented on herself, and she didn't like what she found. As Robert Fulford reports:

She set aside enough time to re-read a book she had loved as a young woman, Hermann Hesse's Magister Ludi. *Alas, she soon discovered that Hesse no longer pleased her. "I hated the book. I hated the whole so-called experiment." The narrative proved painfully slow.*

She had changed in ways she would never have predicted. "I now read on the surface and very quickly; in fact, I read too fast to comprehend deeper levels, which forced me constantly to go back and re-read the same sentence over and over with increasing frustration." She had lost the cognitive patience that once sustained her in reading such narratives.

She still buys books, "but more and more I read in them rather than being whisked away by them." At some point she had "begun to read more to be informed than to be immersed, much less to be transported."

She's not alone. As a writer in the Guardian *recently pointed out, "Skim reading is the new normal." Just about everyone does it, perhaps not aware that in a few years it becomes habitual. The reader who skims can lose the ability to grasp another person's feelings or perceive beauty.*

I've had similar experiences myself. A few years ago, I noticed that I really enjoyed reading on airplanes and wondered why. After a bit of reflection, I realized that it was because I wasn't distracted by the temptation to check a device every now and then, allowing reading to be the kind of immersive experience I once took for granted. Now I make a point of semi-disconnecting every night, sitting down with a novel and a glass of wine, with my computer and phone out of reach. I try to do the same thing when I'm reading for work instead of pleasure, setting my devices aside so that I can read deeply and really think about things but it's always a struggle. And I don't think that I'm alone.

I'm not suggesting something as simplistic as books good, Internet bad. There's nothing inherently good about books as such – *Das Kapital* and *Mein Kampf* are both books with murderous consequences, and books that obviously did nothing to improve their readers' critical-thinking abilities. But the capacity for deep reading and deep thinking is a valuable one, and one that is being tossed aside for no particular reason. As Fulford notes, "Universities report that students now avoid signing on for classes in 19th-century literature. They realize they can no longer work through Dickens or George Eliot."

In his classic *The System of Freedom of Expression,* Yale First Amendment scholar Thomas Emerson wrote:

> *Freedom of expression is an essential process for examining knowledge and discovering truth. An individual who seeks knowledge and truth must hear all sides of the question, consider all alternatives, test his judgment by exposing it to opposition, and make full use of different minds. Discussion must be kept open no matter how certainly true an accepted opinion may seem to be; many of the most widely acknowledged truths have turned out to be erroneous....*
>
> *Freedom of expression is essential to provide for participation in decision making by all members of society. This is particularly significant for political decisions. Once one accepts the premise of the Declaration of Independence – that governments "derive their just powers from the consent of the governed" – it follows that the governed must, in order to exercise their right of consent, have full freedom of expression*

Social media is addictive by design. The companies involved put enormous amounts of thought and effort into making it that way, so that people will be glued to their screens.

both in forming individual judgments and in forming the common judgment.

The kind of deep, wide-ranging, multipolar community debate that Emerson envisioned as key to our system of freedom of expression is at odds with the surface-skimming, tribal, catchphrase-based nature of social media. In a recent piece, Daniel Hannan suggests that our politics are becoming more vicious because we're becoming stupider – as a result of social media shrinking our attention spans:

The fall in IQ scores in the West is perhaps the most under-reported story of our era. For most of the twentieth century, IQ rose by around three points per decade globally, probably because of better nutrition. But that trend has recently gone into reverse in developed countries.

You hadn't heard? I'm not surprised. Journalists and politicians won't go near the subject and you can see why. Consider the theories offered by neuroscientists for the decline. Some argued it had to do with the rising age of motherhood, because the children of older mothers tend to have lower IQs, other things being equal. No one likes to say this, because it can come across as "older moms have dumb kids," which is not true. (My wife and I were 44 when our youngest child was born, and my own parents were also elderly, but that didn't make me too thick to grasp the concept of statistical distributions.)

Other theories were even more explosive. For example, that unintelligent people were having more kids, or that the fall in average scores reflected immigration from places with lower IQs.

But a new study from Norway, which examines IQ scores from 730,000 men (standardized tests are part of military service there) disproves all these ideas, because it shows IQ dropping within the same families. Men born in 1991 score, on average, five points lower than men born in 1975. There must, in other words, be an environmental explanation, and the chronology throws up a clear suspect: the rise in screen-time.

Kids brought up with Facebook and Instagram are more politically bigoted, not because they don't hear alternative opinions, but because they don't learn the

concentration necessary to listen to opponents – a dif-
ficult and unnatural skill.

It's unfortunate that social media not only makes such debate more difficult on its platforms, but also, it seems, rewires people's brains in such a fashion as to make such debate more difficult everywhere else. It is made worse by the fact that Twitter in particular seems to be most heavily used by the very people – pundits, political journalists, the intelligentsia – most vital to the sort of debate that Emerson saw as essential.

In fact, the corruption of the political/intellectual class by social media is particularly serious, since their descent into thoughtless polarization can then spread to the rest of the population, even that large part that doesn't use social media itself, through traditional channels. Writing on why Twitter is worse than it seems, David French observes that even though its user base is smaller than most other social media, those users are particularly influential:

But in public influence it punches far above its weight. Why? Because it's where cultural kingmakers congre- gate, and thus where conventional wisdom is formed and shaped – often instantly and thoughtlessly.

In other words, Twitter is where the people who care the most spend their time. The disproportionate influence of microbursts of instant public comments from a curated set of people these influencers follow shapes their writing and thinking and conduct way beyond the platform.

It's tempting, when reading a news feed full of rage and hysteria, to console yourself in the knowledge that it's "just Twitter." But behind those angry, hyperbolic tweets (well, the blue-check-marked ones, anyway) are people, and those people are disproportionately the most engaged and most influential men and women in American public life. It's "just" the American political class putting its rage and intemperance on display, hoping to remake the world in its own irate image. And the surprising success of that attempted makeover should scare you, whatever your own political views are.

Twitter is also the most stripped-down of the social media platforms, and thus the most illustrative of social media's basic flaws. Just as sad people repetitively pulling the levers on gas-station slot machines illustrate the essence of gambling without the distracting glamour of casinos and racetracks, so Twitter, without a focus on "friends" or photos, or other sidelines, displays raw online human political nature at its worst. This makes it easy for people to get worse.

You can reject Twitter's toxicity by leaving the platform, as I did in the fall of 2018. But French is right that this doesn't really solve the problem: "Absent large-scale collective action by the political/media class to reject the platform, simply logging off Twitter is merely a *personal* defensive mechanism – a sometimes necessary mental-health break that all too often correlates with diminished influence in the national political debate." With Twitter, you can participate and be driven crazy – or you can stay sane, and lose influence. That's a bad trade-off.

Too Emotional

In *The Shallows,* Nicholas Carr writes:

> One thing is very clear: If, knowing what we know today about the brain's plasticity, you were to set out to invent a medium that would rewire our mental circuits as quickly and thoroughly as possible, you would probably end up designing something that looks and works a lot like the Internet. It's not just that we tend to use the Net regularly, even obsessively. It's that the Net delivers precisely the kind of sensory and cognitive

*stimuli – repetitive, intensive, interactive, addictive –
that have been shown to result in strong and rapid
alterations in brain circuits and functions. With the
exception of alphabets and number systems, the Net
may be the single most powerful mind-altering technology that has ever come into general use.*

*The Net also provides a high-speed system for
delivering responses and rewards – "positive reinforce-
ments" in psychological terms – which encourage the
repetition of both physical and mental actions. When
we click a link, we get something new to look at and
evaluate. When we Google a keyword, we receive, in
the blink of an eye, a list of interesting information to
appraise. When we send a text or an instant message
or an e-mail, we often get a reply in a matter of seconds
or minutes. When we use Facebook, we attract new
friends or form closer bonds with old ones. When we
send a tweet through Twitter, we gain new followers....
The Net's interactivity gives us powerful new tools for
finding information, expressing ourselves, and con-
versing with others. It also turns us into lab rats constantly pressing levers to get tiny pellets of social or
intellectual nourishment. The Net commands our
attention with far greater insistency than our television or radio or morning newspapers ever did.*

Social media is addictive by design. The companies involved put enormous amounts of thought and effort into making it that way, so that people will be glued to their screens. As much as they're selling anything, they're selling the "dopamine hit" that people experience when they get a "like" or a "share" or some other response to their action. We've reached the point where there are not merely articles in places like *Psychology Today* and *The Washington Post* on dealing with "social media addiction," but even scholarly papers in medical journals with titles like "The relationship between addictive use of social media and video games and symptoms of psychiatric disorders: A large scale cross-sectional study." As mentioned earlier, one of the consulting companies in the business of making applications addictive is even named Dopamine Labs, making no bones about what's going on.

As Adam Alter writes in his book *Irresistible: The Rise of Addictive Technology and the Business of Keeping Us Hooked,* addictive technology is big money. And the consequences are severe:

> *Kids aren't born craving tech, but they come to see it as indispensable. By the time they enter middle school, their social lives migrate from the real world to the digital world. All day, every day, they share hundreds*

of millions of photos on Instagram and billions of text messages. They don't have the option of taking a break, because this is where they come for validation and friendship.

Online interactions aren't just different from real-world interactions; they're measurably worse. Humans learn empathy and understanding by watching how

People are more likely to believe misinformation on social media because they tend to only read headlines that mesh with their preconceived ideas, and they tend to get and share those headlines from friends, family, or people they see as ideological allies.

their actions affect other people. Empathy can't flourish without immediate feedback, and it's a very slow-developing skill. One analysis of seventy-two studies found that empathy has declined among college students between 1979 and 2009. They're less likely to take the perspective of other people, and show less concern for others. The problem is bad among boys, but it's worse among girls....

Many teens refuse to communicate on the phone or face-to-face, and they conduct their fights by text. "It's too awkward in person," one girl told Steiner-Adair.

"I was just in a fight with someone and I was texting them and I asked, 'Can I call you, or can we video chat?' and they were like 'No.'"... That's obviously a terrible way to learn to communicate, because it dis- courages directness.

It's also a terrible way to learn empathy, as the emotional response to one's behavior, normally displayed in things like facial expressions, body language, and tone of voice, is reduced to text and emojis. Perhaps this is one of the reasons for the shame mobs: To the mobs, their targets don't really seem human. But while the shame mobs throw their stones in a sort of play, their victims' lives and careers are ruined in earnest.

Essentially, the addictive aspects of social media (and other online apps) are intended to bypass the conscious thought process and go directly to the limbic system, after the fashion of many drugs and intoxicants, or, for that mat- ter, of gambling. That's not new, of course – people in bib- lical times drank wine and gambled, and it wasn't new then – but the methodology is. The fact that this stimula- tion is being achieved via technology, rather than by old- fashioned methods, makes it more reminiscent of the "direct limbic stimulation" advertisements that inflicted an unquenchable thirst for "Mokie-Coke" in Frederick Pohl's

dystopian novel of advertising excess, *The Merchant Wars*.
It is a case of "behavioral addiction," rather than chemical
dependence. (As Sherry Turkle writes, "The machine's
prowess was exploiting our vulnerabilities: we wanted to
feel recognized, and we didn't want to feel alone.")

Nor is this addiction limited to young people. In fact,
as a recent article in *Wired* by Clive Thompson reported,
the evidence is that older people – the middle-aged Gen-
eration Xers in particular – are the most hooked:

> *The data suggests that the ones most hooked on their*
> *devices are those graying Gen Xers. Research by Niel-*
> *sen, for example, found that Americans aged 35 to 49*
> *used social media 40 minutes more each week than*
> *those aged 18 to 34. Gen Xers were also more likely*
> *than millennials to pull their phones out at the dinner*
> *table. (Baby boomers were even worse!) The middle-*
> *aged spend more time than millennials on every type*
> *of device – phone, computer, tablet – and, while they*
> *don't peek at their phones while driving more than*
> *young people, they do it more than they should.*

Historically, of course, we've regulated addictive products,
whether drugs, liquor, tobacco, or gambling, more strictly
than other products precisely because addiction, by its

nature, overrides people's reason and works directly on desire. Social media companies may come to be regarded more like tobacco companies than like media companies, with consonant calls for stricter regulation of their products, or at least the addictive aspects thereof. Likewise, one argument for regulating porn or violence in entertainment is that those forms go straight to the limbic system, arousing emotions without any intervening thought or argument. The comparison to Twitter seems pretty obvious.

Too Untrustworthy

"A lie," as an old aphorism has it, "can get halfway around the world before the truth gets its boots on." In the world of social media, this statement may actually turn out to be overoptimistic. It sometimes seems as if the lie gets halfway around the galaxy before the truth gets its boots on.

Even before social media, of course, it was a standard joke (stemming from an ancient *New Yorker* cartoon by Peter Steiner) that "on the Internet, nobody knows you're a dog." Social media only amplifies this tendency. First, setting up an actual website (say, a blog or a news site) takes a modicum of effort. Not a huge amount, but some. Setting up a social media account, on the other hand, takes less than a minute. You're then free to be fake. That's one reason why Twitter and Facebook are plagued by fake accounts to the point that they've instituted "verified" statuses for celebrities, so that people can be sure that the person they're following is the real deal. But what about the rest of us? A fake celebrity is nice, but dozens – or hundreds, or thousands – of fake "bot" accounts purporting to be ordinary people can give the impression that an idea is gaining traction when it's all manufactured.

Sometimes it can swing elections. In the very close Alabama Senate special election between Roy Moore and Doug Jones, donors supporting the victor, Jones, used a false-flag "Dry Alabama" campaign to convince people that Moore wanted to ban alcohol. The Daily Caller reported:

> *Operatives with New Knowledge, a group affiliated with Dickerson, created thousands of Twitter accounts posing as Russian bots to boost the election-year chances of Jones – the accounts began following Moore's Twitter account in October 2017. The project created a slew of Facebook accounts as well that were designed to troll conservatives into opposing Moore.*
>
> *But the misinformation project attracted attention from local and national media, falsely suggesting Russia was backing Moore's candidacy.* The Montgomery Advertiser, *for one, was the first to cover the story*

using the Russian-bot angle. National media outlets
quickly followed suit.

"Roy Moore flooded with fake Russian Twitter fol-
lowers," read the headline on a New York Post *story,*
which cited the Advertiser. WaPo *focused its reporting*
on the fact that Moore blamed Democrats for the fake
accounts. Other major national outlets picked up on
the story shortly thereafter, with many pundits mock-
ing Moore for blaming Democratic operatives.

But it doesn't take a six-figure campaign to spread misinformation on social media. Even fairly obvious parody accounts
are often taken as real and quoted by real-life news media:
The "DPRK News Service" Twitter account, purporting to
be a North Korean media outlet, has fooled CNN, Fox News,
Newsweek, and other major outlets into reporting its content as if it were a genuine product of the North Korean
government. Though to be fair, as Gizmodo reported a while
back, that's partly because "many of the tweets are only
about 10 percent more ludicrous than the real English-
language news feed of North Korea."

People are more likely to believe misinformation on
social media because they tend to only read headlines that
mesh with their preconceived ideas, and they tend to get
and share those headlines from friends, family, or people

they see as ideological allies. This makes them less critical and more willing to pass on things that on further thought they would probably recognize as bogus. In addition, of course, social media passes along only tiny niblets of information, allowing and even encouraging people to make assumptions about the background, assumptions that also tend to follow their preconceptions and prejudices.

The Argument for Regulation

Unsurprisingly, the characteristics of social media outlined above have produced calls for regulation. As a form of media that is addictive, mentally damaging, and prone to spread misinformation – all while allowing giant corporations to form detailed dossiers on our likes, dislikes, and connections – social media raises numerous concerns, many of them legitimate.

Traditionally, we've regulated private information like credit info and health records. We've – until recently, at

As a social media user, you face the paradox that people harassing you can be anonymous, even as you have no privacy from the social media company, or from anyone who can hack, or buy, your personal information.

least – regulated pornography and other forms of what the Supreme Court calls "low value" speech. We've regulated substances, like drugs and tobacco, and practices, like gambling, that promote addiction and dependence. And (again until recently) we've regulated false and defamatory speech in terms of libel and slander.

As Andrew Arnold writes in *Forbes*:

> *Some of the strongest proponents of social media argue that it is a matter of public interest to regulate social media. They say that regulating it may be as important as regulating tobacco or alcohol. One of the arguments they make is that social media empowers large corporations to control the flow of information. As long as they can afford to saturate social media feeds with posts that curate the information they want, anyone standing in opposition to that is essentially steamrolled because they don't have the resources to counter that.*
>
> *It isn't only businesses that may benefit at the expense of the consumer. It can also be governments vs. citizens. Oppressive regimes such as the one in the Philippines or Russia appear to be using social media as a tool in their efforts to remain in power.*
>
> *There's even a health aspect to consider. With constant notifications and pressure to never miss the next*

viral post or bit of information, social media platforms
are using the same techniques that casinos use to draw
in gamblers. Considering that most platforms are
open to people from the age of 13 on, that's troubling.

The pressure for regulation is certainly growing. Some of this is fallout from the 2016 election: The fable that "fake news" or "Russian bots" swung the election is mostly a comforting myth for Hillary Clinton supporters still groping to explain their loss. As researchers from Princeton and NYU who explored the phenomenon of "fake news" on social media found, it's "important to be clear about how rare this behavior is on social platforms.... The vast majority of Facebook users in our data did not share any articles from fake news domains in 2016 at all."

And, of course, just because fake news attacks didn't swing the last election doesn't mean they won't be a threat in the future. As dependence on social media increases, and as techniques for manipulating opinions grow more refined, the likelihood that foreign actors – or domestic ones, as in the Alabama Senate special election mentioned earlier – will change enough peoples' minds to flip an election grows higher.

There are also serious concerns about privacy, with Facebook's data breaches, and scandals at other providers, demonstrating that loss of privacy is baked into the system as it currently exists. As a social media user, you face the paradox that people harassing you can be anonymous, even as you have no privacy from the social media company, or from anyone who can hack, or buy, your personal information.

In addition, existing companies like Facebook have started to embrace the idea of some sort of regulation. This isn't necessarily to be applauded – established companies tend to favor regulation of their industries as it makes life harder for new entrants who might be potential competitors. And it's a safe bet that whatever regulation Facebook favors won't do much to limit Facebook's freedom of action, or to impose any sort of genuine accountability for misbehavior. Still, with less industry opposition, some sort of regulation becomes more likely.

Types of Social Media Regulation

But what kind? There have been numerous proposals, but here are some of the most significant:

End online anonymity: Trolls, bots, and cyberstalkers take advantage of anonymity online. Thus, the argument goes, we should end anonymity, or at least limit it. As one proposal, summarized by Mark Courtney in AccountingWeb, has it:

We believe that anonymity is important, but if some-thing goes wrong, there also must be some way to get back to the source. This doesn't mean that people always have to be overtly identifiable, and it would certainly be hard to regulate, but we would recom-mend a responsible body or trade organization where the authorities (closely controlled) would be able to track illegal activity back to its perpetrator.

Here's an analogy we like to use: People should be able to travel the Internet highway with the equivalent of a car registration plate that's issued upon proper verification by a secure and certified issuing body or identity provider – just like a car registration.

While the registration could be used to identify you if needed, the sites you visit on the Internet wouldn't need to know your name or where you live, unless you wanted to tell them your details (give con-sent). And if you wanted to hide your appearance from them, then that would be possible too.

However, just like the real highway, if there's an issue, such as speeding or dangerous driving, a repu-table body would be able to trace the incident back to the culprit with confidence. Although, hopefully, it wouldn't come to this very often, the fact this could happen would provide assurance to others on that highway (and their parents) and would ensure that drivers act more responsibly. This would allow the beneficial aspects of anonymity, yet take away the perceived sense of being untouchable, which can cause so much damage.

It's been a bad few years for "reputable authorities," alas, and I don't know who I'd be willing to trust with this sort of power. But that's the least of it. The notion of requiring a license to speak on the Internet – because this is effectively what's being proposed – raises the possibility of people's licenses being revoked, a matter with obvious concerns for freedom of speech, and freedom in general. This sort of a regime was imagined in Vernor Vinge's *True Names*, and that story was a cautionary tale, not a how-to manual.

Remove Section 230 immunity: Under Section 230 of the Communications Decency Act, Internet publishers are not responsible for the content of information that comes from "another information content provider." Initially, this was meant to protect against, for example, newspapers being held liable for libelous statements by their readers in comment sections. Now, however, it protects services like Facebook or Twitter from liability for effectively everything on their sites, since everything there is content provided

Besides, the rather sorry state of "fact-checking" journalistic enterprises suggests that unpopular opinions will be treated as incorrect facts, and popular opinions as the reverse, on a fairly regular basis.

by someone else. It's doubtful that these sites could survive in the absence of Section 230 immunity. If you wanted to force a return to something more like the old blogosphere, a widely distributed network of small publishers, then this repeal would likely accomplish that end, though the repeal of Section 230 immunity seems highly unlikely, given its impact and the opposition it would create. Basically every major tech company, every social media company, and every traditional media company would be in opposition. Perhaps lesser tweaks might be possible, say requiring due care to prevent the spread of false or defamatory or threatening information, but it would be an uphill battle.

More scrutiny of users: The chief approach that the social media giants have taken so far has been to ban people who say things they don't like. This has resulted in people like Infowars' Alex Jones being banned from Twitter, and an extremely unsuccessful effort by Tumblr to ban pornographic content, as well as the regular "Facebook jailing" of people who post political content that offends Facebook's in-house censors. The problem is that this censorship seems to fall much more heavily on the right than on the left, given the – extremely – left-leaning makeup of the social media companies' workforce.

In an interview last year, Twitter's CEO Jack Dorsey admitted that his company is "left leaning," but denied that it affected the company's policies. In a separate interview with NYU Professor Jay Rosen, Dorsey admitted that some conservatives who work at Twitter "don't feel safe to express their opinions at the company." Dorsey said he thought that was wrong, and that everyone in the company should feel free to express their opinions, but if Twitter's employees aren't safe expressing non-lefty opinions, what of Twitter users?

This sort of one-sided censorship is one of the reasons, together with the other concerns mentioned here, why I deactivated my Twitter account. Censoring people is always going to be ideologically fraught, and social media companies are apparently incapable of addressing this in an unbiased manner. At any rate, seriously throttling destructive content would probably cost them a lot of money. As Jaron Lanier writes, "A social media company is in a better position if it doesn't know what's going on, because then it makes just as much money but with less culpability."

More scrutiny of content: Writing in *The Hill,* Anders Aslund argues that "each social media company should be obligated to establish a system for checking incoming information and exclude what is obviously false or even slanderous. Fact checking is not enough. Sheer lies must be expelled. Wikipedia has done so voluntarily, and it should be in the interest of the social media companies to do the same."

Well, the history of my own Wikipedia entry – which at one point, among other things, featured a photoshopped picture of me in an "I had an abortion" T-shirt as if it were real – leaves me skeptical about how good a job Wikipedia has actually done. And it, too, has shown rather extreme political bias. But there are only two ways this kind of fact-checking can be accomplished on a social media platform. Either everything has to be checked when it's posted, an impossible task, or things have to be checked when there are sufficient complaints, which is as likely to encourage mobbing and targeting of political opponents as anything else. Besides, the rather sorry state of "fact-checking" journalistic enterprises suggests that unpopular opinions will be treated as incorrect facts, and popular opinions as the reverse, on a fairly regular basis.

Algorithmic transparency: Social media all offers us "curated" content, which means, basically, content chosen to manipulate us and hold our attention. This is accomplished via algorithms, which are deep secrets. Similar algorithms are, and would be, employed to control "undesirable" speech. But how do they work? Do they work? As York University Professor Natasha Kusikov writes in *The Conversation*: "Is 'trust us' a good enough response, given the problem? With so much at stake, it may be time for a fundamental rethink of how these indispensable 21st century companies are regulated and what they're allowed to do. At the very minimum, governments and citizens should reconsider whether the lack of oversight into how these companies shape our speech rights is really in the public interest."

Facebook already experimented with manipulating voter turnout. As Jaron Lanier writes: "In the published research, Facebook used the cheerful example of boosting voter turnout. But since Facebook is all about targeting and can calculate your political affiliation, among many other things, and since it has also proven it can make people sad, it is likely that social networks can also be used to suppress voters who have been targeted because of how they are likely to vote."

Algorithmic transparency would limit that to some degree. So would a mandatory "vanilla" algorithm. When Facebook was new, it just showed you what your friends posted, in the order they posted it, with no algorithmic jiggery-pokery. I strongly preferred that, and one fairly nonintrusive form of regulation would be to require something like that as an easy-to-activate option. Facebook would hate this, because jiggery-pokery is their business model, but it wouldn't be hard to implement. Some people might choose to let Facebook manipulate their feed, but even those people would, if this were implemented transparently, always be aware that Facebook was engaging in that manipulation.

As part of algorithmic transparency, or in addition to it, regulators might target aspects of social media specifically designed to be addictive. Not only do we traditionally regulate addictive substances ranging from alcohol to heroin, but we also regulate addictive behaviors like gambling. And, as with those other addictions, there's arguably a public-safety angle: Addiction to social media can lead to distracted driving and other unsafe behavior, as well as inattention to work, relationships, etc. A study of social media users aged 19–32 by researchers at the University of Pittsburgh School of Medicine found much higher rates of depression among the heaviest users. (We've even seen "neurobiological programming" to respond to smartphone notices used as a courtroom defense to charges of distracted driving, though so far unsuccessfully.) Given that companies invest substantial effort and money into making their apps addictive, it seems as if there's something to regulate there. And, in fact, Anne Longfield, the Children's Commissioner of England, has called for such regulation already in the UK, with support from Health Secretary Jeremy Hunt.

Most of these forms of regulation at least potentially raise First Amendment issues, even to the question of "curating" feeds. How those issues might ultimately be resolved is beyond the scope of my discussion here, and

Knowing nothing makes you easy to manipulate. Lack of relevant life experience makes you easy to manipulate. So maybe people should know more?

may turn out to be quite sticky: Can Facebook or Twitter persuasively claim First Amendment rights as publishers while simultaneously seeking Section 230 immunity by claiming that the things they publish come from someone else?

And leaving aside the First Amendment discussion, which tends to devolve into a technical argument about what courts will do, there is the broader free speech argument. Free speech in America is, or at least has been, a cultural value, not merely a narrow legal one. And the calls for regulation are a problem that way. As Peter Suderman writes in *The New York Times,* "Given the unanticipated reach and influence of these companies, this view is perhaps understandable. But it is mistaken and even dangerous, because at its core it is a view that speech – the primary use for these platforms – is not an individual right, but a collective good that should be subject to political control." He's absolutely right about that, which is why I favor other approaches to regulating social media – though I note that social media companies themselves seem to regard the speech of their users as a collective good subject to their own control.

Other Approaches

Leaving aside various forms of content regulation, is there anything else that can or should be done? Well, we might better achieve the goals of regulation by regulating something other than speech. Although antitrust is out of fashion, the huge tech companies constitute interlocking monopolies in various fields, and often support one another against competitors – as Paypal, for example, cut off money transfers to YouTube competitor BitChute, and Twitter competitor Gab.

And, more significantly for our purposes, it's the walled-garden character of these services, coupled with their monopoly status, that brings many of the dangers people complain about. When destructive content goes on Twitter or Facebook, or when cascading waves of hysteria hit these services, they can spread to the limit of their user base. But if Twitter or Facebook were competing with five or ten other similar services, or maybe even two or three, this sort of thing would be more likely to damp out, after the fashion of the old, loosely coupled blogosphere. In addition, competition would promote greater attention to matters of privacy, algorithmic integrity, and so on because users could more easily leave for another service. Right now, if you don't like Facebook or Twitter, there's no substantial alternative, and if you decide to leave Facebook for Instagram, you're just leaving for another Facebook property with a slightly different user interface.

Antitrust regulation would also dilute the political power of these big companies, and that's a real issue. Old-time monopolies like those broken up by Teddy Roosevelt concentrated economic power (in industries like railroads, steel, or oil) and gained political power as a result. But the very nature of social media companies' monopolies amplifies their political power even before they start hiring lobbyists. As Columbia Law Professor Tim Wu notes in his new book, *The Curse of Bigness: Antitrust in the New Gilded Age,* "industry concentration leads to political corruption: Big monopolies aren't just an economic threat: They're a political threat. Because they're largely free of market constraints, they don't have to put all their energy into making a better product for less money. Instead, they put a lot of their energy into political manipulation to protect their monopoly."

An industry made up of 500 companies might want government protection, but it's harder to get them to agree on a lobbying campaign. One made up of three companies, or one, can do so, and be sure that it will reap all the rewards of its effort.

Thus, as Wu notes, "The more concentrated the industry, the more corrupt we can expect the political process to be." And, as he points out, these fears (and the realities) of huge companies wielding unchecked political power motivated the antitrust crusaders of a century ago every bit as much as concern about prices. (As the first Justice John Marshall Harlan wrote to his former law partner Augustus Willson in 1905, "Indeed, the greatest injury to the integrity of our social organization comes from the enormous power of corporations. We must have corporations. We could not get along without them, but we must see that they do not corrupt our government and its institutions.")

In total, Wu reports, "Facebook managed to string

together 67 unchallenged acquisitions, which seems impressive unless you consider that Amazon undertook 91 and Google got away with 214 (a few of which were conditioned). In this way, the tech industry became essentially composed of just a few giant trusts: Google for search and related industries, Facebook for social media, Amazon for online commerce."

And these new tech monsters have a one-two punch that Standard Oil lacked: not only do they control immense wealth and important industries, but their fields of operation – which give them enormous control over communications, including communications about politics – also give them direct political power that in many ways exceeds that of previous monopolies.

As Wu writes: "Big tech is ubiquitous, seems to know too much about us, and seems to have too much power over what we see, hear, do, and even feel. It has reignited debates over who really rules, when the decisions of just a few people have great influence over everyone."

Rather than focusing on the content of what individuals post on social media, regulators might better focus on breaking up these behemoths, policing anticompetitive collusion among them, and in general ensuring that their powers are not abused. This approach, rooted in antitrust law, would raise no First Amendment or free speech problems, and would address many of the most significant complaints about social media.

Building Immunity

As I mentioned early on in talking about early cities and disease, the easy spread of pathogens was one factor, but another was malnutrition. Poorly nourished populations tended to do much worse in the face of epidemics than those that were well fed. There is probably an analogy in the social media world too.

People succumb to disinformation or mass hysteria in part because they're predisposed to. But what predis-

> **Almost always, the organization's reaction is channeled through social media specialists, and social media specialists are the *very* last people who are going to tell their bosses that it's safe to ignore social media. But, in fact, it usually is.**

poses them? Well, some of it's just being human: We're all emotional beings to one degree or another, and all of us are capable of getting irrational in the right circumstances. But just as everyone can get sick, some people are more resistant to disease than others, so there may be some things we can do to boost people's resistance to the downsides of social media. So maybe we should nourish people's minds and make them more resistant.

Mental Nutrition

In bragging about how he manipulated the political news media, Obama foreign policy advisor Ben Rhodes described them this way: "Most of the outlets are reporting on world events from Washington. The average reporter we talk to is 27 years old, and their only reporting experience consists of being around political campaigns. That's a sea change. They literally know nothing."

Knowing nothing makes you easy to manipulate. Lack of relevant life experience makes you easy to manipulate. So maybe people should know more?

I've written elsewhere about the failures of our educational system, but in a time when two-thirds of millennials don't know what Auschwitz is, it's not crazy to think that our populace could be toughened up when it comes to mental nutrition. Basic knowledge of civics is poor, knowledge of history is limited and politicized, and the once-traditional canon of western literature, myth, and philosophy no longer holds sway. People who know more – note, not necessarily people who are "more educated" in the contemporary sense – are harder to fool. If we wanted a populace that was more resistant to propaganda and hysteria, we'd be educating people better. So why aren't we?

Defensive Memes

Short of reforming the entire educational system – a noble goal, but a big one – is there anything else we can do? Well, short-term education in critical thinking would be helpful. When I was in an enrichment class in elementary school, they taught us using The Propaganda Game, a component of Layman Allen's educational games. The Propaganda Game explained different types of propaganda ploys, then presented various efforts in which we were supposed to identify the techniques being used. I remember recognizing those techniques all over major media after that. Updating this approach to the current day probably wouldn't be hard – there's an online version of The Propaganda Game now – and exposing as many people as possible to it would be useful.

That sort of education would be very helpful today, I think. News stories often suggest that today's youth are "savvy consumers" of Internet news, but there's more evidence for the "consumers" part than for the "savvy." Training people in critical reading and critical thinking would go a long way toward minimizing the danger of social media misinformation and hysteria. It seems to me that the educational system in the mid-20th century, when social media was entirely unforeseen, trained people better for skepticism and thoughtfulness than the educational system today, when social media is everywhere.

And perhaps, like ancient cities that didn't understand the germ theory of disease but nonetheless acquired decent sanitation by rule of thumb, we will come upon some social arrangements that will reduce, if not eliminate, the dangers of social media. Generally speaking, human societies find a way to deal with new challenges. It is likely that we will do the same with social media, or perhaps that the evolution of communications technology will leave social media as obsolete as the telegraph, leaving its problems behind – in exchange, no doubt, for an entirely new batch.

Acquired Resistance

And no doubt people will learn on their own. As recounted earlier, Jon Ronson started out enthusiastic about Twitter shame mobs – they seemed anti-hierarchical and democratic. But after a while, they seemed more mobby and cruel. As the excitement wears off, we can expect social media to be viewed differently. And in my own observation, younger people seem less enthusiastic, and more fearful, of social media than people did a few years ago when Facebook and Twitter were new. As I write this, Facebook and Twitter seem to be stagnating in terms of new users, and some see them facing potential financial problems in the future.

As early cities grew, people gradually adapted to the disease environment – or perhaps more accurately, the people with weaker immune systems died off and failed to reproduce – and the population over time became more resistant to disease. Diseases didn't go away, but they went from epidemic to endemic, with once-lethal plagues reduced to tolerable childhood diseases.

The Power of Doing Nothing

Perhaps we'll achieve a similar state with regard to social media. And perhaps the most productive path to such immunity and adaptation is the realization that what happens on social media isn't actually that important. There is a strong sense in which, as Noah Millman wrote in *The Week* recently, what happens on Twitter isn't real. Millman comments:

> *When Twitter "blows up" in response to something controversial associated with the organization, does*

that demand a forthright response to prevent serious harm to the organization's reputation? And how can you predict in advance what will spark such a storm?

It's extremely hard to know — because Twitter, like the financial markets, is also a chaotic system, and hence inherently unpredictable. In the face of that uncertainty, the default for many organizations is to react defensively, but it's not clear that defensiveness is effective, in either the short or long term....

What if they followed a PR strategy that presumed that, in the Twitter era, the baseline level of negative publicity is always going to be higher than it used to be — and that the presumption should be that the publicity has few real consequences in monetary terms. Firing off an angry tweet is the second-easiest thing in the world to do, the only thing easier being liking someone else's angry tweet. If that's all that's happening, then what's happening really isn't real.

Millman notes that *The New York Times* followed such a strategy when it faced demands to fire columnist Ross Douthat over a column sympathetic to the old WASP aristocracy. At one level, he notes, it suggests the *Times* supports Douthat. But, he observes:

In another sense, though, what it suggests is that the
Times is confident that a wave of Twitter outrage is not
actually a threat to their bottom line. Their readers may
write nasty comments, but they aren't actually going
to leave. In fact, they don't even actually want Douthat
to leave, because the opportunity to vent their outrage
is part of the experience they came for, whether they
actually read his piece or just heard about it on Twitter.

I think there is deep wisdom in this approach. Social media (especially Twitter) is full of sound and fury, but usually it signifies, well, not much. People are angry on social media (especially Twitter) in no small part because so many people go there in order to be angry. Once the anger is discharged online, it's very unusual for people to actually follow it up with concrete actions in the real world.

One reason why social media has the impact it has is because the people who run big organizations grant it more power than it really possesses. Lots of journalists are on Twitter and write about it (after all, writing about what happens on Twitter doesn't even require you to leave your office or make a phone call, and the quotes are already online, ready to cut and paste). With that coverage, what happens on social media *seems* important. And at every big organization, whether it's a corporation, a government agency, or a university, there's now some sort of social media specialist. Almost always, the organization's reaction is channeled through social media specialists, and social media specialists are the *very last* people who are going to tell their bosses that it's safe to ignore social media. But, in fact, it usually is.

If organizations routinely imposed a three-day or seven-day waiting period on responding to social media storms, they'd usually find – and by "usually," I mean "almost always" – that by the time the waiting period had passed the outrage mob would be gone, distracted by the next shiny object. (Or the one after that.)

It's also a good idea to have principles. If you have a rule like "we don't fire people over social media posts," then you don't have to engage and explain each case. (Or, for that matter, if you have a rule like "employees aren't allowed to use social media.") Without rules, you find yourself trying to make explanations to a mob that doesn't want explanations, only capitulation. And your capitulation, likely as not, will just set off an opposite-but-equal mob angry that you gave in.

Widespread adoption of these principles would substantially tame the Twitter outrage mobs. Like two-year-olds, they scream in no small part because they know someone is listening. If you want to continue the disease analogy,

The presumption is that, overall, truth will win out most of the time. The danger of monopoly organs like Facebook or Twitter is that they will selectively silence some of those voices and amplify others.

social media is like those diseases that kill by causing the victim's own immune system to go into overdrive. A less fevered response might be healthier.

As for reducing the spread of misinformation, well, that will take more than inaction. The ignorance of the average voter, rational or otherwise, is of long standing, and a review of newspapers from our nation's first century will not reveal any Golden Age of sober, nonpartisan factuality. And already, the widespread reporting on "fake news" has presumably encouraged people to be at least moderately more skeptical of what they see and read online.

At any rate, here, too, breakups seem in order. The "marketplace of ideas" approach to free political speech has always relied on a wide variety of different views from a wide variety of different speakers, many of which will inevitably be wrong or even dishonest. The presumption is that, overall, truth will win out most of the time. The danger of monopoly organs like Facebook or Twitter is that they will selectively silence some of those voices and amplify others. Encouraging these tech behemoths to police "bad" content only makes that more likely.

With a greater diversity of social media platforms, the risk of systemic bias – the sort that's most likely to steer elections, and society, in a particular direction via falsehoods – is reduced. With more platforms, more news can filter through the cracks, and people can compare coverage from one to another. (This is especially true if, as they should be, antitrust laws are applied to prevent collusion among platform providers.) With people's attention split among more platforms, too, chain-reaction hysteria will be reduced.

Conclusion

And that, in a way, is the bottom line. Policing the content of social media speech, beyond a very basic level of blocking viruses and the like, is a bad idea. The more involved and granular the policing becomes, the worse of an idea it is, because it looks more and more like political censorship, which is what it will inevitably become.

Policing platforms, and collusion among them, however, is likely to do more good than censorship. Antitrust scrutiny of monopolies and collusion will do more for the integrity of social media, and the protection of society from hysteria and misinformation, than regulation of content. And such antitrust regulation doesn't raise the same First Amendment and free speech problems.

An approach based on antitrust and competition will preserve free speech while reducing social media abuses. As social media grows more pervasive, and more obviously destructive, the pressure for regulation is sure to grow. Better to regulate in a way that preserves free speech, and that doesn't empower tech oligarchs.

First American edition published in 2019 by Encounter Books,
an activity of Encounter for Culture and Education, Inc.,
a nonprofit, tax exempt corporation.
Encounter Books website address: www.encounterbooks.com

Manufactured in the United States and printed on acid-free paper.
The paper used in this publication meets the minimum requirements of
ANSI/NISO Z39.48–1992 (R 1997) (*Permanence of Paper*).

FIRST AMERICAN EDITION

LIBRARY OF CONGRESS CATALOGING-IN-PUBLICATION DATA
IS AVAILABLE

10 9 8 7 6 5 4 3 2 1